Men Want To

Exhale Too

PJ PETERSON

First published 2009 edited by Mary Stinyard

Republished 2012 edited by Kitty Kennedy

Formatted using Microsoft Office
Printed and bound in the United States of America
by CreateSpace, Inc.
www.createspace.com

DEDICATIONS

■ □ ■

First and foremost I want to give thanks to God for creating me, blessing me, and giving me the talent to do the things I do.

■ □ ■

To my line brothers 9 F.S.O.P, my chapter Lambda Phi (HARD PHI), the Upsilon Sigma chapter(MIGHTY US), and the greatest fraternity in the world, OMEGA PSI PHI FRATERNTIY INC.

■ □ ■

To every woman that has ever blessed this earth with her presence, may you know that real men understand that it is the essence of a woman that illuminates our existence and purpose in life.

■ □ ■

To my rock, my inspiration, my heart, my perfect compliment.

■ □ ■

To my father, Edward E. Peterson and my mother, Shirley A. Cruse. I love you both dearly and miss you every second of my life. R.I.P to you both until we join again.

■ □ ■

The Message

Many times in a man's life, he wonders if he will ever really meet that special someone. At some point he wants to find that particular person who is the breath of his very essence. When it comes to finding the perfect compliment, a man sometimes feels that he looks when no one is there, and sometimes he is there when no one is looking. In the same manner that a woman seeks her mate, a man wants to find that significant individual that completes him. It seems that in the world today, men are not given enough credit for the good things they accomplish. Contrary to some belief, there are good fathers in the world. There are single parent men who do an excellent job at raising children, as well as those who are great mentors to the youth. Though it appears to be portrayed in society that all men are dogs, it is the tenacity of the dog that instills the quality of perseverance in men. It must be reestablished that the world possesses not only good men, but great men. It must also be established that a man can love a woman with tenderness and understanding just as a woman loves a man. The great ones get

4

overlooked and the good ones get underestimated, therefore the wrong ones are most often chosen. Just as well as the woman wants the best and feels that she is sometimes wronged, the man has the same virtues and values. You can not do a book report without reading the book. Cliff's notes will not help. So, until you get to know that man with a complete sense of understanding… Please do not stereotype him, because a man wants to exhale too!

Chapter 1

He is a man of success, influence and humility. A man that works every day from 9am-5pm; The CEO and founder of Self Help Innovative Technology, or as some refer to it, the S.H.I.T. Though it sounds funny, the firm grosses 6.6 billion dollars a year. Now that is the S.H.I.T we would all work for. Standing at 6'4 and dark complexioned, he has a fresh shaven head that shines brighter than the afternoon sun, nice goatee, with a body that appears as if sculpted by the Greek gods themselves. He sports a fresh crisp tailored made suit each day and a distinctive scent of cologne that when he walks by, women pause as they slowly inhale his intoxicating pheromone. He embodies what every woman fantasizes about: single, no children, great shape, wealthy and highly educated. Dr. Melvin Arthur Nobles is his name. Academically, Melvin was a top honor student, receiving his Bachelors and Master's degree from Fort Valley State University and his Doctorate from Howard University; a spirited alumnus that gives back to his prestigious institutions. Dr. Nobles is the kind of man that is loved by everyone. He is not only a valued professional, but also a great mentor and a well-respected figure throughout his community. It seems that everything is perfect in his life. Well, almost everything.

Aside from his mother, there is no woman present. Dr. Nobles is very near and dear to his parents. He has spent so much time being a great son and doing for others that he's never really taken the time to enjoy his own social life. How could this be so? Every woman that knows him personally or even laid eyes on him has wanted him, as if there is a genetic organ that keeps him above the rest of mankind in women's eyes. He is the perfect catch. So why is he single? Why not be a player with all his wealth? Thing about it is, Melvin never really paid attention to women as relationship figures even though he has always been the perfect gentleman. Melvin knew that with his trust in God and his faith in the word, one day an angel shall be delivered to him. Not because of his accolades but because of who he is as a man. His mother taught him the business side of life. His father taught him how to be a man, the importance of respect and how to cherish a woman. These lessons were instilled in Melvin so that he would be prepared for the day he would be blessed with the gift of a soul mate.

One day Dr. Nobles was looking out over the city of Atlanta from his 66th floor office window just thinking to himself about what life would be like with a companion. Melvin then looked across the streets of the Atlanta, closed his eyes and took a deep breath. Before he could exhale, there was a sudden knock at the door. He turned around and there entered the most beautiful woman that he had ever laid eyes on. She stood about 5'3, pecan red tan, hazel eyes, micro braids, and a pair of legs that were so bowlegged; it looked like she was riding a horse. Her skin was honey glazed and a voice soft as a whisper. This was a true delivery from heaven.

Chapter 2

Melvin has no idea that standing before him in his office was not only a beautiful woman but an independent woman. She is of strong stature, determination, and possesses the will to put her best foot forward and excel in the professional world. She is a woman who has not only experienced the joys of life, but a woman who has been through it all, enduring the pain of being looked down upon by society's stereotypical eyes. Here stood a woman who is determined to prove to the world that she is a prominent figure to reckon with. But she is also on a quest, in search of a void that she has been looking for her entire life.

"Excuse me, excuse me."

"I am looking for Dr. Melvin A. Nobles, the secretary at the front desk said that I could find him up here."

"Are you Dr. Melvin, Sir?"

Melvin was in awe by the beauty that this woman who had just walked into his office radiated. As she stood there with an inquiring smile on her face, he stood there emotionless as if he was dumbfounded. Then finally after a second of mental hesitation he exclaimed, "Yes!"

After realizing he sounded like a kid on Christmas, he calmed down and returned to his professional state.

"Yes, I am Dr. Nobles, how may I help you?"

"Well actually you might not remember me but I attended Fort Valley State University at the same time you did. As a matter of fact we took a couple of courses together, but you probably never noticed me because you were always the outspoken type that everyone loved. I was more of the shy type and didn't really say much to anyone. I usually sat in the back of the class and kept my head in the books. When it was time to leave class, I was gone before anyone could notice there was a person sitting in the desk that I occupied. I tried to stay out of the limelight. After my freshman year, many people tried to hate on me and labeled me a freak. So when I got the chance, I moved off of campus and isolated myself from the public eye. I never really hung around. I was tired of people labeling me and they never really knew me, just hating basically because I was what they wanted to be, more or less."

"As I recall, your senior year was my sophomore year and we were on the Honda Campus All Star Challenge Quiz Bowl Team together." Melvin pondered the thought for a second and then he yelled, "Yeah... yeah I remember, Angel, right?" With a smile that could stretch across the peninsula.

"Yes, you remember me!" She responded with joy.

"You were labeled?" He asked.

"I never heard anything about you. Actually, I use to think that you were kind of attractive."

"Kind of?" she asked.

"Well, you know what I mean, you were attractive"

"Were? You mean like in the past tense?" She responded to him as if they were on jeopardy.

"No, no, not were, was. I mean is, are, hell you look good girl, that's what I am trying to say!" Finally he gets it out with conviction.

"You were the quiet type though, as I can remember you were highly intelligent."

"Were?" She asked again.

"No, no" nervously speaking again, "not were, was, I mean is, are, hell you are a very intelligent woman to my knowledge." As Melvin baffled through his statements of recollection, he laid his eyes on her beautiful body. Her sexiness enraged a sexual prowess inside him that had not been awoken his whole life. "So what brings you to the top floor, to find me?" Melvin asked. "Well, I am kind of embarrassed to say. I was engaged to this high-class lawyer in New York. We were about a week from getting married. He was working late trying to close this case that had been hung for about a month. So I figured that I would surprise my man, and bring a romantic evening to him." Angel sat down in the chair next to her as tears ran down her adorable cheekbones. "As I approached his office door to surprise him, the door just pushed right open as if he was waiting for me. So I walked in timidly forgetting the reason I was there and wondering if something was wrong. I walked into the office and there he was." Angel is crying big crocodile tears at this point. Melvin anticipates that she is about

13

to tell him the worst news a person can get. He knows in his heart that she is about to tell him that her fiancée is dead, so he walks to her to console her. She looks up at Dr. Nobles and says "sitting at the desk with his head back motionless. Not saying a word, the body was limp and loose as if he were beaten by the police in the LA Riots. At first, I didn't know what to say, I just looked with sorrow. Then it happened. I belted out, Lord why! His eyes suddenly opened as he sat up straight in shock and then" Melvin grew with anticipation, "then…" Melvin was on the edge of his seat. Angel looked up at Melvin, grabbed his hand firm and said, "It was the janitor."   "Huh?" Melvin exclaimed.

"The janitor," she said. "The janitor was under the desk performing oral pleasures to my man. He was a feminine looking man, and well you know what, just ughh" she expressed. Dr. Nobles heard this and did not know what to say after that. He just found out that this dime piece in front of him had a fiancé who had a boyfriend.

"What the fuck?" Melvin blurted out loud.

14

Angel began to laugh hysterically. Once Melvin realized that it was a joke he began to laugh uncontrollably also. After a moment of laughter, Melvin began to gain his composure. "So, what really brings you to my city? You know, this is a big change from Fort Valley. In Fort Valley, we were content with it being small, quiet and rural even though it was a great place to live. This is a place that moves a lot faster and never sleeps. I do recall you being the quiet type, and usually those type of people are used to and comfortable with the slower pace of life. You know, the laid back, countryside, wake up and watch the sun rise type of living; As opposed to the fast track, bright city lights, got to get it before the sun rises type of city."

"Hmm!" she exclaimed. "You don't know me. You don't have any idea what I have been through. You don't know what I am capable of and what I can achieve. You're just a man, a man who has power. See a man like you thinks that he knows everything about a woman. Look at you, standing there in your suit and tie, with your CEO title. I'm sure you got all these women

running around here thinking they can be the first Mrs. Nobles."
Angel started walking toward Melvin with a black woman's
swagger like she just proved to the whole world that her man was
no good and she exposed him on a daytime talk show

"Fuck that." emphatically speaking.

"Let me tell you something. I am a woman. I am the future.
I am the pinnacle of excellence that every man desires. I am the
backbone that holds every hard working man together when he
needs support. See, I don't need you to tell me where I am or
where you think I can fit in. I need you to fear me. Fear the fact
that I am a strong black woman. Fear the fact that at any given
moment it can be my office, my firm, and my franchise business
that you, "the man" need a recommendation for. It is my essence of
being a woman, my prerogative that you cannot handle, yet you try
to understand on a daily basis. So don't assume that I can not
handle this city, assume that this city can not handle me." Melvin
now looks like a deer caught in the headlights. He has nothing to
say and nowhere to go. Melvin feels as if he just walked into a

civil rights room for black women against prejudice and he was the first Klan president. Right as it seemed that Angel had put Melvin in his place she broke down. "I'm sorry" crying harder than a midget at Six Flags. "I'm sorry, I can't help it. I had a relapse and I was just thinking about...about. Don't worry about it." Melvin comes closer to comfort her. "What? What is it Angel? What are you trying to say?" "It's just that my last boyfriend abused me. He said that I was no good and that I was not the ideal woman. He accused me of working too much and thought that I should be at home, barefoot and pregnant. He could not stand the fact that I was independent. He thought that because he was the man in the house, that he was the man of the house. Until one day, I came home and he had been drinking. I tried to leave but yet, he began to beat, hit, and throw me around the house until I escaped his grasp. I kicked him as hard as I could where the marbles are not made of stone. Once he dropped to his knees, I got out of there faster than a 35-year-old virgin in his first piece. See, I came to Atlanta to start over. To find a man who will love me for me and accept my ways.

17

I want a man who will say to me the things I need to hear and not just want to hear. Then and only then will I feel as if I am complete." As she finishes her testimony to Melvin, she slowly looks up into his charming eyes and begins to gaze. He reaches out to her slowly, and lightly rubs the side of her face with his strong yet gentle hands. He lightly swipes the top of her cheek bone down to her chin, pulling her in closely to his lips, and then kisses her on her cheek. Then in the most romantic and comforting way, he says, "Relax. You are where you need to be, and you need to be where you are. The rest is up to you and me. I appreciate who you truly are."

THOUGHTS for the MIND PART I

SEX vs. Sex

A man walks onto a car lot. Of course he sees all these nice cars for sale, but there is one in particular that catches his eye. It's a jet black LEXUS sitting on 24's with the frog light eyes. It's clean as a new born baby rinse. He walks up to it and feels how smooth the paint job is. He can imagine himself inside this LEXUS all day every day. He stands back and just says to himself 'HELL Yeah' this me all day, and the price is affordable. He pulls out his money quick and tells the dealer "here you go", gives the dealer the money and buys this piece of work. Now that it is his he grabs the keys, opens the door, jumps in the car, and rides away happy. BUT, as he drives off he glances at the back seat and notices the seats are a little damaged, but thinks to himself, "ah, that's ok". Then he notices that the seatbelts don't work. "Hmm, no protection? Ah that's ok". Then he notices the radio has a short in it. Now he gets a little perturbed. So when he gets home he really starts to see what this great looking car really is worth. He sits for a minute and notices the glove box is jammed. The mats on the floor are covering a hole where you can see the ground. There is a small mildew smell coming from the back of the car that he didn't notice until he really just paid attention. So now he is pissed. He turns the car on and takes it back to the dealer. The dealer points out to the man, the AS IS clause. What you see is what you get. The dealer explains to the man that you saw what you wanted to and decided the purchase this car. I did not have to sell you anything. I will take it back this time but you get no refund. You would have noticed all the things wrong with the car on the inside if you had only took time to learn the car, instead of just jumping into it. Honestly, that is how I make my money. Every man I know usually just jumps right in without taking the time to learn it. A lot of people make the mistake of getting what they think is best instead of learning what they should know is best. In today's society we move fast without really knowing the proper technique of running. This is why athletes cramp up because they do not take the time to properly train and stretch. The reason we fail tests and quizzes because we do not study and we rely on cheating or cutting corners to get the job done. Basically, we compensate things and situations for the instant gratification of satisfaction as opposed to thoroughly analyzing our process of enduring what we want to eventually paramount into the word called love.

A partner's Sex, as in MALE or FEMALE, cannot be determined over night. I cannot learn or clearly understand the true value of a woman's Sex or gender without getting to know her first. I can claim to have appreciation for her without her physical stimulation as a satisfaction. I feel in order to truly be stimulated by her Sex and not her SEX; I must be able to depict the characteristics of her well being as a woman. I must be able to mentally stimulate and challenge her thought process and combine it with passionate building blocks to proceed to a potential bond of what is called love that will lead to an impeccable hopefully everlasting love with endless romance, love, and SEX. But first I

21

must learn her Sex. To appreciate someone is to value them. Some people value may value SEX, but it has no value. But when a person values the Sex of a person, then the value of the person's SEX will eventually then become priceless.

I am not saying that SEX is not ok and I am not saying that it is ok. I am saying that people need to start understanding the difference of values. Yes SEX may be good and feels great but when the value of it runs out, you get bored and move on and compensate with more SEX and more SEX, until one day you will be dispensed out and no one wants that LEXUS. It will look good but will have a low value, where basically anyone can afford it. BUT, if you put your Sex first, you make the other person define your character and understand who you are and the value of your Sex. The sad thing about this note is a lot of you may agree and some may be mad, but most of you will continue to have SEX just as frequent and maybe more after you read this and will miss the point. Some of you will not even care and still wonder why your value is not high, though you may think or "know" you are the bomb. Wake up people. Learn each other's Sex before you learn each other's SEX.

Chapter 3

As the sun shines through the black silk curtains, the rays bounce off of her well structured physique. She rolls over slowly and moans softly as if she was in an Herbal Essence commercial. Her face looks just as cherubic as it did when she laid to rest the night before, and she wakes up and finding herself alone in a bed softer than a feather filled pool. Angel begins to look around for Melvin but does not see him. She then rises out of bed and puts on a nice silk robe lying beside the bed. Confused by the isolation, Angel travels into the living room. She stops and finds what she feels is the most beautifully sculpted man she had ever laid her eyes on; sleeping on the couch like a new born baby. From top to bottom Angel scans Melvin as if he were a roll back item at Wal-Mart. She looks at this amazing man with a mind to tear into him like a new box of chocolate covered strawberries. She drifts for a minute in a deep thought of pure ecstasy, wondering what making love to this unique male species would be like. She begins to perspire with erotic anticipation of what could come of this sexy prowess that is lying asleep before her. Angel's mind starts to wonder into a fantasy world of forbidden pleasures. Suddenly, he begins moving slowly, ascending into an upright position, allowing his feet to touch the floor. Not fully awaken, Melvin rises from the couch with his eyes half open and stands tall with a stretch so wide, his muscular definition is clearly visible from head to toe. Angel catches a Kodak moment of Melvin's nice looking tool that she fantasizes fixing her plumbing. He then opens his eyes and is surprised by Angel standing there. Melvin quickly grabs the throw pillow, which barely hides his manhood, and covers his personal being. "I'm sorry, didn't know you were standing there." Standing in a great appreciated daze, Angel is completely speechless. It seems as if she has not heard a word Melvin has said. "I hope you slept well. Last night I tucked you in and made sure that you were comfortable. I came out here and slept on the couch. I wanted you to know that I am a gentleman. Sure you are beautiful, but the process of participation is enhanced by the reality of anticipation. You are a diamond princess, one whose beauty can not be measured by words, but by the actions of my politeness. I want you to feel comfortable. I want you to know that in our world satisfaction is of the mind and your beauty is of the heart. My mind may tell me to satisfy this beautiful woman, but my heart says value this lady. Treat this lady as the soft pink pedal in a garden of black roses."

"The words that form from my lips are as pure as the glow from your skin. I want to one day immerse you in the true spirit of passion, but first I must anoint you in the world of a gentleman." As the words flow form Melvin's mouth like sweet poetry, Angel has not heard a word. She is still stunned by this magnificent piece that she has viewed behind the pillow. Stuttering in a baffled daze, "Did, did, did you say something?" Melvin chuckles to himself as if he can't believe that he is pouring his heart out this woman and her mind is somewhere else. "Hmm, it's okay. I know that if you heard me you would be cool, but my heart says you feel me."

Melvin walks over to Angel and pulls her close. He then places his hands around her waist. Kisses her on her nose and softly places his forehead on hers. Looks into her eyes for about six seconds and slowly and softly kisses her on the lips. Melvin then takes Angel by the hand and walks her to the bedroom. He throws back the sheets and lays her down. First he places her on her stomach and takes some honey flavored oil and drips it down her back. He then takes his tongue and slowly starts from the back of her neck and licks down the middle of her spine to the small of her back. He takes his hands and palms each round cheek of hers with his hands. Slowly rubbing each cheek in a circular motion, he gently blows down the crack of her derriere with his warm breath. Rubbing the back of her thighs with his goatee he takes his tongue and slides it from behind into the hidden warmth of her thighs. She reaches back and grabs Melvin's bald head. The deeper he slides his tongue inside, her body begins to arch and she rises up on her knees. Melvin's face is now pressed firmly against her soft buttocks. He then turns over onto his back with his tongue still inside her warm pink palace. As he lies down flat, he slowly pulls her down onto it. She begins to rub his head and ride his tongue back and forth as if she was a jokey in the Kentucky Derby, securing his face between her inner thighs. Melvin takes his lips and begins to massage her clit firmly and suck on the tip of it. His tongue probes her lips back and forth until her climatic tunnel is open and flooding with ecstasy. Melvin sucks, pulls, and massages all of Angel's juices into his mouth, not allowing even one drop to escape. After about 45 minutes of ultimate oral stimulation, Melvin lays Angel on her back and slowly pulls out his tool, preparing to enter her warm embrace. He teases the tip of her erotic zone until she is shaking hysterically. He then slowly slides his love muscle inside of Angel inch by inch until she feels that nothing else really matters. He is inside her with the perfect fit. She feels that his tool is the piece that fits her long awaited erotic puzzle. With the slightest strokes of his rod of thunder, Melvin opens the floodgates of pleasure to angel's thighs, overflowing with her own juices. Eye to eye they look, though she can not focus. Her eyes roll back and

28

forth, and her body is thrust into space mountain frenzy. He tries to kiss her as he makes dynamic love to her but she is so busy trying to breathe that she just can't take it. Finally, after a couple hours of pleasure and pain Melvin is about to discharge. He grabs her tightly and she knows that he is about to explode. Her loud moans and sexiness is about to send Melvin's secretions into a volcanic eruption. Faster he goes with anticipation of ejaculation; Melvin belts out with a loud "Grrr", and tidal waves like a 20 year tsunami. Panting, moaning, and gasping for air they both fall asleep in their pool of wet ecstasy. Knowing that he has just put it down, Melvin dozes off with a smile. Knowing that she just had her mind blown like never before, Angel passes out with a smile on her face and between her thighs. The aroma of Love Spell and Mambo for Men both permeate the room. Melvin has put his princess on a throne above all clouds.

About 30 minutes have passed and for some strange reason Melvin cannot sleep. He is not sure if Angel is awake or not, but the deep passionate thoughts of what has just occurred is replaying in Melvin's mind like a cinematic romance that has no end. With that being said, Melvin finds his hand slowly rubbing his shaft softly at first, trying not to disturb Angel, as he figures she is resting pleasantly. Little does Melvin know that on the other side of this ecstasy filled bed Angel is indeed awake. She is also replaying the same erotic scene over and over in her mind as if there is no level greater. She feels the movement in the bed and suspects that Dr. Nobles is touching himself and longs for him to satisfy the uncontrollable throbbing inside her. So without hesitation Angel gives out a soft moan just loud enough for Melvin to hear her. Completely turned on by this arousing sound, Melvin's tool begins to straighten as if it were standing at attention. Melvin keeps his right hand on his manhood and takes his left hand, gently laying it on her stomach. He then slides his hand between her thighs finding a place that is hotter than the core of the sun, but ironically cool and wet as the ocean, capable of eradicating any type of heat. He slides his hands slowly between her flesh and begins to fondle her love lips with his fingertips. As she begins to

30

moan on a repeated basis, he keeps his fingers rotating in her love palace while she watches him stroke his shaft for her. He then proceeds to take his hand and rub her love lips completely as he inserts his magic fingers inside her. Now that she is back in a place that she just left, Melvin takes his whole hand and palms her love nest, rubbing on it with a rhythmic speed that is sure to cause climatic arousal. He rolls over and looks her in her eyes, licks his lips, rubs a little faster and places his manhood on her thighs sliding it aimlessly against her skin. Reaching over to the side of the bed, he grabs the baby oil from the night stand. While he is still rubbing on her, giving her uncontrollable emotions, he drips the baby oil onto her thighs. Now he begins to use the oil as if it was paint and his tool as the brush. Back and forth he strokes his brush romantically while he inserts his fingers in and out or her love zone. Melvin then rises out of the bed and picks Angel up in the air and carries her outside onto the balcony to enjoy the summer rain. As he carries Angel across the room on his face, he blows on her tender lips gently and kisses on the inside of her thighs. He begins to tease her clitoris with the tip of his tongue, but does not go as far as inserting it in her cave dwelling. He methodically paces through the living room with Angel in hand. Slowly he pauses and places her against the wall for more of his passionate oral display. He then slides her down the wall gently with his tongue climbs her body. They begin to kiss and hold each other tight. Caught up in a passionate display of kissing they find themselves moving throughout the house onto the balcony. Melvin stands Angel against the rail and spreads her legs as if she were under a sexual arrest. He slow dances with her from behind as if they were in the club. His hard on dangles between her soft cheeks, as he kisses her on her neck, and reaches between her legs to again rub on her love palace. As the rain comes down faster, Melvin begins to rub on her faster and kiss on her neck. Then, he softens the touch of his fingers as he probes them deeper inside her, rotating his fingers simultaneously. Reaching back to grab his manhood, Angel grabs his girth with a tight grip of pure romance. As the rain is coming down, he is rubbing on his woman with complete eroticism, she is stroking his tool with a fast pace, and she feels her love zone about to erupt. Faster, harder, and deeper he goes, rubbing, kissing, and licking his woman. All of a sudden," I'm coming!" she exclaims. Melvin drops down to his knees instantly and begins to suck on her wet and steamy insides from behind. This move sends her into complete orgasmic ecstasy. She explodes into his mouth and he proceeds to catch all of her milky nectar with the flow of the rain. He sucks on her clitoris harder as she climaxes guaranteeing complete satisfaction. As her knees buckle and she limps over the rail with a gasp of air, Melvin arises from his knees, picks her up, and as a woman crossing the threshold, he carries her back to the bedroom. He then lays Angel in the bed, fluffs her pillow, and pulls the sheets over her to comfort his lady. Angel lays her head on Melvin's chest as he lay next to her, staring directly into his eyes and simply smiles.

Chapter 4

"Mmmm" Angel moans and stretches as she wakes up from a night of erotic passion. "Wake up baby, baby wake up. Great morning, Mr. Nobles or might I even say hell of a night that was with you, Dr. Nobles!" Angel exclaims emphatically with a smile. "Good morning, my beautiful Angel." Melvin gently says to his cherubic companion with a smile and a slight rub across her cheek. "I must say, that was a beautiful night last night. Though, I feel as if I were not good enough. I feel as if I did not satisfy you completely." "What?" Angel interjects. "Man if you don't go somewhere with that non sense. I am still throbbing. I can't walk. I feel like I have no bodily fluids left. That was the most exhilarating night of passion of my life." "Okay, okay I get it." Melvin laughs as he understands Angel's reaction. "I must go to the office and take care of some things. We have a big time corporate meeting coming up in a week that I must prepare for. Sweetheart, if I make this sale, we will be set for life."

"Oh we will huh?" Angel replies.

"So, you are saying that one, we will be together and two, that you feel I am going to be content with you making all the money." Melvin looks in awe and thinks to himself; oh man here we go again. "Melvin, I want you to know that I plan on advancing my career at S.H.I.T and being just as powerful as you. Not because I am your lady, but because I am a woman of excellence and prestige. I will work, learn, and network my way to the top just as well as any hard-working, determined woman would. I promise that one day you will see me in the business world as a mogul. Like Jay Z said 'I'm not a businessman, I'm a Business, man." Angel and Melvin chuckle to the hip hop reference. "Seriously sweetheart, I just want you to know that I am determined to be the best I can be, for me. So I can be proud of myself. And if you are happy for me, than that is an additional blessing, but Melvin I will succeed for me. I have struggled too long and too hard not to."

Melvin walks over to his lady and holds her close,"Baby, I know that you will be the best at what you do. I expect nothing less. I hope that you do advance in the company as well as my life. You know how much you mean to me. I am not trying to say that I will be the sole provider but I will be your soul provider. I am yours yesterday, today, and forever." He kisses her on the cheek, the forehead, and the lips and holds her tight. As an hour goes by Melvin is at work diligently putting together his proposal for this upcoming sales pitch. He gets a knock on the door. Enters a woman in a long black dress with heals to match. Her dress has a split up one side where you could slightly see the curviness of her buttocks. This was a very beautiful woman. "Hello." she says in a seductive manner.

"My name is Honey. I am the sweetest thing that you will ever meet."

She walks over to Melvin slowly like a cat on the prowl. "I heard that you were the man of the year." Honey sits down in front of Melvin's desk and crosses her long beautiful legs slowly as if she were trying to hypnotize him with her beauty. She begins to speak with a sexy sarcastic tone. "Dr.Nobles, Mr. Nobles, Melvin the man. How can you help me? Or better yet, how can we help each other?" Melvin looks at the woman with a peculiar look as if he does not know her. "Lady, I don't know you and I don't know what you are talking about. But it seems to me that your intentions are not of my liking. So if you do not have a serious issue, concern, or business plan, I am going to have to ask you to excuse yourself. With that being said, what is the nature of your business?" The lady rises out of her chair slowly and begins to move toward Melvin. She walks behind him as he faces forward in his executive chair. She takes her cell phone and she makes a call. "Come on in girl, I got him." Melvin hears this and jumps out of his chair faster than a rabbit having sex.

"Whoa, Whoa, Whoa!"

"What the hell is going on here?" I am a happy man. I have a girlfriend who I love dearly and would never..." and before he could finish his statement Angel walks in. "Shut up Melvin. I love you too, now sit down, and be quiet!" Melvin has a complete

look of confusion. Angel walks in with a white sun dress on that is

sheer enough that Melvin can see the outline of her sexy body.

Angel walks up to Melvin and pushes him back down in the chair.

"Now baby, I know what you have given me thus far; I can't be

anything less than satisfied. So now, I want to surprise you and do

something special for you." Still with a baffled look on his face,

Melvin sits back in his chair and anticipates what is to come.

Angel approaches Honey in a manner that has Melvin confused yet

to his surprise, stimulating. Angel takes her hands and stands

behind Honey, slowly sliding her hands from her ankles up to her

thighs, feeling between the split in her dress. She then proceeds to

move with Honey in a dancing like motion back in forth in front of

Melvin while he gazes on in a childlike excitement. Seductively

the ladies dance and feel one another in front of Melvin as if they

were making love to one another standing up. Angel moves closer

to Melvin and begins to kiss him as Honey begins to give him a lap

dance out of this world. Melvin feels as if he were in heaven. He sits back in his chair and watches the woman undress each other as Angel tells Melvin to lay back and close his eyes. Like a school kid in Pre-K, Melvin follows his instructions and closes his eyes and then all of a sudden… "Wake up baby, baby wake up. Great morning to you, Mr. Nobles." Melvin jumps out of his sleep confused only to realize he had been dreaming the whole time. Melvin leans over to Angel with a laugh and kisses her on the cheek. "Good morning to you my beauty."

Chapter 5

Melvin gets out of bed and takes a shower as he prepares himself for his day at work. While in the shower, he hears a beeping noise. It appears that Angel's cell phone is in the bathroom. "Oh, she must have left this in here by accident," he says to himself. Melvin grabs the cell phone to take it to her. Right before he exits the bathroom he thinks to himself, "hmm I don't want to invade her privacy, but…, what the hell!" He looks down onto her screen and there is a message. *Hello boo, how are you? I miss you and I can't wait to see you again. Call me!* This text message has Melvin pondering the thought of deception. So Melvin begins to go through all of the text messages he can. He finds different little messages such as, *Hey boo, what you been up to? I miss you boo! I had a great time last weekend. You know you are the best.* As Melvin views each text he begins to encompass himself into a sea of depression. He begins to think to himself all

the wrong things. He begins to suspect that Angel has another.
Being the type of man Melvin is, he figures to himself that he has
to step his game up even more in order to captivate this precious
woman whom he adores.

After a few tears and a slight pain in his heart, Melvin
wipes his face dry and walks out of the bathroom back into the
bedroom placing her phone on the night stand without her noticing.
Melvin walks around to his side of the bed and sits down slowly.
Angel rolls over, sits up, and places her hands across Melvin's
back and begins to massage his shoulders. "Hey baby, how you
feeling this morning? You feel a little tense," she exclaims to
Melvin. As he sits on the edge of the bed with his head slightly
hanging down, he responds to her in a mild fashion "Oh nothing,
I'm good, just a lot on my mind that's all. I will be alright." He
then turn around, gives her a hug and embraces her as if she was
the last person on earth. "Wow, baby I just want to say last night
was amazing. I could only imagine ever being loved like that.
Melvin Nobles you are the man!" Melvin hears Angel's

compliments, but on the inside all he can do is think of the messages that he has just read in Angel's phone. "Baby." Melvin says with a low and saddened voice. "Let me ask you a question and I hope you will be real with me. Will you promise to always be honest with me no matter what?" Angel sits by his side and holds him close with a little concern and replies, "Of course sweetheart, I care for you and will always be honest with you, no matter what." She takes his hands and holds them gently rubbing the back of his hands softly. "Why do you ask, is there something wrong? Is there something on your mind you want to talk about?" At this moment, knowing he should say something about the text messages, Melvin looks angel in the eyes and says, "No sweetheart, I believe you", then kisses her on the forehead and gets up to prepare himself for work.

As he gets in his car and proceeds to pull off for work Melvin turns the radio down and begins to pray *"Lord, I hope that with your guidance and will, all things will be good between Angel and I. I really care for her and believe she is the one. Whatever she has done in the past is in the past. But her present and future is what I hope to be a part of. Please lord give me the strength to persevere through any obstacles that I must, to show my Angel that I am the only man she needs. In your name, Amen"* Melvin releases a deep sigh and turns his radio off and drives to work.

Chapter 6

Angel drinks the orange juice from her glass and grabs a piece of toast with a dab of jelly spread across it and heads out the door to corporate America. She slides into her 2009 Lexus with leather seats. She lets the roof back on her custom designed convertible as the wind blows through her micros briskly. She listens to some old school Luther Vandross as she goes to work. Angel gets to work and parks her car in her nice executive spot. As she gets out the car, her fellow colleagues stare in awe of her beauty and whisper to each other how lucky Melvin is to have such a beauty by his side. Angel grabs her briefcase and then walks across the parking lot into the building as if she were a cinematic masterpiece. As she rides the elevator up to her office floor, she steps off the elevator and speaks to everyone cordially as she always does. Just as friendly and well liked by her colleagues as her man, Angel smiles all the way into her office. Once Angel

44

arrives at her office, she walks in and closes the door. She kicks off her heels and sits back in her chair and gazes out the window. Angel begins to stretch like a human letter X when the phone rings.

"Hello, this is Angel, how may I help you?" as professional and customer service friendly as can be.

"Girl what you doing?" Her best friend asks.

"Just another day in the office girl, you know how it is!" Angel exclaims to her best friend on the phone.

"Girl, let me tell you. Melvin is the best thing that has ever happen to me. I mean really, he is kind, sweet, funny, and very professional. When we are at work, it is strictly professional. I mean I don't mind at all. It kind of turns me on to see my man in a suit and tie every day making power decisions that benefit the company and me". She chuckles.

"Everyone in the corporation loves him. He is a genuine catch. I know that a lot of women believe their man is the one, but sweetheart, he is definitely the one. Sometimes I wish that I would have never been the way I was back in school. I wish I was as pure as the sunshine on Easter Sunday. But you know girl, we all have our past."

"I feel you on that Gel." Her friend responds.

Angel sits back in her office chair and stairs out the window as she begins to think about her past. "Girl, you know when we were in school people use to talk about me and say things that they really had no idea of. Now I will be the first to admit now that I did my thing and had my time at being promiscuous but all in all, I feel I turned out good. I think when I went to party, the clothes I wore and my carefree attitude stamped me in a negative way. People never really knew what was going on with me though. Like most haters in the world, they just assumed what they wanted. It is a shame what college life can do to a persons self esteem if they let it. But the one thing I will always remember is Mr. Peterson's favorite line. 'Yesterday was a memory, tomorrow is a blessing, but today is a gift and that is why we call it the present.' Girl, you know that stuck with me for some reason. No matter what other people thought or said, I made the best of what I had.

My first couple of years I would let the pettiness get to me. But

through my matriculation of years, I learned to grow in faith of

myself and not worry about words. I had to learn from my

mistakes and transcend them into positive accomplishments. Why

is it that beautiful girls are always the most hated? Yes, I have nice

curves, yes my skin is soft, and yes my smile is to die for." She

said with a small chuckle. "But why must I be ridiculed? Why

must the guys who have all the women, be players; but a girl like

me who has many guys chasing me have to be considered a hoe? I

never really did anything with any of them. Yes, I flirted a lot and

may have teased a few. Ok, maybe all of them, but was I wrong?

Why does it have to be that way? Huh? Hello? Hello!?" exclaims

Angel. Angel sits up and listens to the phone only to realize the

dial tone. She look at the clock and realize that she has been

rambling on and on for about twenty minutes. She looks on her

desk and sees the light flashing on her personal cell phone. There

is a text message from her best friend. *Girl, I tried to tell you that I had to go, but you were just talking and talking as you do best,*

LMAO. I know that when you get this message you will lol.

Anyway, I am glad you found the one. Don't let him go! You know

us women tend to let the good one's go or just have them as good

friends not realizing they are the one until it is too late. Girl, you

realize it now, so keep your head up and be happy. TTYL.

Angel laughs to herself and resumes back to work.

After a couple hours at work Angel receives an instant message on her screen. *Where we going for lunch?* Angel responds, *Doesn't matter to me.* Melvin walks through the door with a hand basket and a bottle of wine. Following him he has a couple of guys in the office dressed in tuxedo's carrying white cloths and wine glasses. As Angel is paralyzed with anticipation, he walks up to her desk and kneels down. He places the basket on the desk and pulls out a fresh salad for her that she loves the most. He then removes the cloth from the chaperone and places it in Angel's lap. He pours the wine into the glass slowly and methodically. Having her salad already made the way she likes it,

Melvin feeds it to her slowly with a sensual politeness. He then wraps his arms around hers as they simultaneously drink the wine. Still not saying a word, Melvin wipes her mouth every so delicately with the cloth, savoring the romance between them. He then stands, bows to his lady, and exits the room leaving just as quiet as he entered her domain. Leaning back in her chair amazed at what has just transpired Angel receives an instant message across her screen. *You are the reason I enjoy coming to work. You are the reason I enjoy life. Your smile is impeccable and your beauty is undeniable. I am proud to be your friend and lover. But most importantly, I am glad to be able to serve you. I remember the night we sat in the living room and just listened to old slow songs. You sat there looking beautiful as ever. Then is when I knew how lucky I was to just be your friend. I feed you nourishment today, as you have fed me oxygen, since the day we met. Angel you are my love!* Angel reads this message and begins to blush and tear up. She immediately runs to the bathroom and wipes her face. After cleaning herself up, she looks in the mirror and says to herself "yesterday was a memory, tomorrow is a blessing, but today is a gift, and I call it Melvin."

Angel returns back to her desk happier than an Olympian winning an 8th gold medal. As she sits down and begins to type on her keyboard, one of the Vice Presidents enters her office. He looks at Angel, smiles and says, "Today must be your lucky day. I am here to tell you that you are moving up. We have been tracking your accomplishments for the corporation and we are highly impressed. You are a valuable asset to this company and we want to show you our appreciation. Starting Monday you will have your own personal secretary and window office. You will be over the Marketing and Communications Division. How do you like that?"

"Do you accept?"

"Yes sir, yes sir, I will take it. Whew!" Angel replies with excitement.

Angel sits back in her chair and is pleased with all of the great things that happened to her today. She begins to smile and thank the Lord for all her blessings. As she picks up the phone to call her best friend to tell her the news, she grabs her chest as a sharp pain runs though like a bolt of lighting. She takes a quick breath. "Are you ok?" her colleague inquires. She then breathes slowly and normally.

"Yeah it's nothing, just excited that's all." She replies.

Though she does not give in to it and treats it as excitement, Angel knows that it's more to it than that.

Chapter 7

Later that evening, Melvin and Angel decide to have a nice quiet meal at the dinner table. Melvin has fixed a home cooked meal for his lovely lady. It is her favorite, fried chicken, macaroni and cheese, green beans, and fresh homemade biscuits with cookie dough ice cream for dessert. As they sit and cherish this beautiful meal together, they listen to some smooth grooves and lovingly smile at each other from across the table. "So how was your day today dear? What did you do at work?" Just as Angel begins to speak; her cell phone rings. Melvin responds, "Oh you can answer it if you like". Angel replies, "It's just a text message, you good. I can text and talk". Melvin smiles and continues his conversation. But as Melvin begins to converse with Angel, he feels as if he is not in existence to her. She is looking at him, but paying more attention and responding to her text messages with smiles and laughter. It is clear that she is drawn to the other party that is texting her. After awhile, Melvin just smiles and removes himself from the table without Angel even knowing that he is gone. Melvin walks into the room and sits on the bed and just hangs his head low and thinks to himself, "I try to do everything so right, but yet it seems that I'm just not good enough. What am I doing wrong?" Melvin decides to walk back into the dining room to be with his love, but when he gets to the corner of the hallway he overhears Angel speaking. "I thought he would never leave. It's like I was trying to hint to him that I was not listening, but he being Melvin, just kept on. I tell you what; meet me at the spot in about thirty minutes. I will tell him something to get away. Ok. Until then, bye." Melvin hears this and does not know how to react. Filled with confusion and hurt Melvin walks back to the room quickly and sits back on the bed as if he knows or has heard nothing. Angel walks into the room. "Melvin my love, I am so sorry. But I just remembered that I need to go to the store and get something for work in the morning." Melvin wants to say something but being who he is he could only respond with, "Yes my dear, I understand." Filled with hurt and betrayal Melvin could not even raise his head to look at Angel as he knows she is going to fulfill her night of deception and betrayal. Angel grabs her purse and exits out the door swiftly.

Arriving at her destination Angel greets her friend with a big hug. "What's up boo, how you been? I missed you! It has been so long. So tell me what have you been up to? How is the business going for you? I know it is very exciting being in the jewelry business!" Angel is so excited to see her old college roommate and best friend. "Girl, you know it has been a long time since we've seen each other. But when I heard you were in town, I had to reconnect with my boo. You know this jewelry business has been great for me. But I heard that you were doing big things over at S.H.I.T. so girl, tell me about this magnificent man you are getting this diamond bracelet for. He has no idea does he?" "Girl no, he has no clue. It was almost a year ago today when Melvin came into my life and I just want to show him appreciation. He is a great man. He is the kind of man that will give me his last dollar, just to see me happy. I have to do this, it is the least I can do. Melvin has been my rock, my friend, and OMG, my lover" They both laugh and high five on that one. "Hell yeah", she repeats "and what a lover he is. Girl I will walk around with a flashlight in the day time searching for that man. He is everything that I ever wanted. So, how you been?" As her friend sits back and smiles she calmly replies, "I have been good, can't really complain. Life has really blessed me since that accident we had in college. Being in this wheelchair has taught me a lot. It has taught me how to appreciate life and all of its blessings. I have a beautiful husband and little girl. They are the center of my life. With that and my faith in God, I will never complain. Life is just beautiful I tell you." Angel grabs her best friends hand with tears running down her face and begins to speak with a sincere voice. "You know I feel ya girl. Ever since that day we were in that accident I thank God that we survived. I have thought of you every day since then and wondered why God did not place me in the same situation as he did you. All I get is these crazy chest pains every now and then. I am sorry girl. I am so sorry that it was you placed in the wheel chair and not me." "Angel, listen. It's ok. You were, are, and always will be my best friend. God has a plan for us all. One door closes but another one opens. I met a beautiful man who loved me for me. I have a beautiful daughter. You have a beautiful man. So here, take this bracelet for your man, my gift to you." Angel is surprised, "But, but, what about the money?" "Angel it's ok. You are my friend. We have both been blessed. And it sounds to me that this Melvin is truly a blessing to you. Take this bracelet as a gift." Eyes full of tears of joy; Angel hugs her best friend and thanks her.

Chapter 8

"Wake up dear! Wake up! "Angel tries to wake Melvin up. Melvin slowly rises and opens his eyes. Angel begins to sing, "Happy Birthday to you, Happy Birthday to you. Ok no more singing". She laughs. "Good morning baby, it is your birthday and I just wanted to make this day your special day. So get up, rise and shine." Melvin rises out of the bed and Angel takes his hand and walks him to the bathroom, which is already hot and steamy from the shower running. As Angel opens the glass door for him to enter she closes it behind him. While Melvin is in the shower she proceeds to the kitchen to fetch the nice breakfast that she has prepared for him. Melvin considers breakfast the most important meal of the day, so she has prepared some of his favorites; crisp bacon, cheesy eggs, cheese grits, pancakes, and toast for her birthday man. Angel places the meal on a tray next to the bed to surprise him when he exits the bathroom. But first, she enters the rest room, drops her robe and enters the shower with Melvin. She places her finger on his lips and says, "Today is your day my king, and begins to bath him slowly and gently in the shower. Kissing him on his chest and massaging him all over gently. After a nice time in the shower, she dries him off and leads him to his meal. Melvin sees this and is in awe. "Baby you didn't have to do this." He opens his arms to pull her in for a strong embrace. Melvin is very appreciative of what his lady has done for him. Later that night, Angel has prepared a special, romantic candle light dinner at home with his favorite jazz musician playing in the background. As they sit at the table and enjoy a nice meal prepared by Angel, Melvin starts to speak, "Baby I appreciate everything you have done for me, but I must confess there is something that has been on my mind." Not knowing how to really say it he pauses for a second. "Baby, I understand but let me say something first please." "Ok dear, ladies first" as polite as a gentleman would respond. Angel gathers herself together and pulls her chair close to Melvin. "Baby, I have known you for awhile now and I am very appreciative of you. I know that it has been a blessing to be with you, and you have done everything for me that you can. You have provided, loved, and cherished me with all your heart. I want you to know that lately I may have seemed secretive but I had to go through an old friend in order for you not to find out what I had planned. I know you know everyone and everyone knows you, so it was hard to keep this from you. But baby," Angel beings to slowly raise a purple box from under the table wrapped in a gold ribbon. "I love you and I want you to know how much you are appreciated, so I give this gift to you on your birthday." Melvin opens the box and views this beautiful diamond filled bracelet with his name spelled out in diamonds. Surprised and relieved by the information that he has just learned, all of his jealous and hurtful thoughts have vanquished. "Now what is it you want to say baby, what has been on your mind?" Melvin looks at Angel and with a deep breath responds,"Sweetheart, I love you and that all that matters. You are truly my perfect compliment!" He gives her a strong embrace and kisses her on her forehead, cheek, and her lips.

Chapter 9

As the days and months go by and the relationship between Melvin and Angel grow stronger and more passionate, Angel is advancing in the corporate world with much growth and productivity. Ten months after being hired at S.H.I.T. She is already the Senior Vice President of Executive Affairs, not to mention she is deeply involved with the CEO of the company. Every year the company has one of the cities biggest end of the year parties in Atlanta. Each year there is a celebrity performance and an employee raffle. This year, the celebrity guest is world renowned entertainer, Jaime Foxx. Jaime performs a plethora of songs from his anticipated upcoming album. The crowd is calm and the mood is peaceful as Mr. Foxx entertains the guests for hours. After Jaime performs, he calms the crowd down around 10:30 pm, and makes the announcement that it is time for the raffle. "Attention everyone! Could I have your attention please?

First of all I would like to thank everyone for coming out tonight

and enjoying this annual festivity. It is indeed a pleasure and an

honor to be this year's special guest. Though I told my boy,

Melvin, that anytime he needs me I'm just a phone call away. But

player, don't think just cause you did this, you on my next album"

the crowd laughs. "Seriously, first I would like to toast to Dr.

Melvin Nobles. Not only is he a great leader, but a great man, and

an even greater friend." The crowd begins to cheer with a loud

uproar. After the crowd begins to quiet back down Jaime proceeds

to announce the winner of this year's raffle. "Ladies and players

who can't afford a date, can I get a drum roll please." The crowd

makes a drum roll noise with their feet and mouths. "The winner

is…is…Angel" The crowd erupts and Angel is shocked. Angel

then proceeds to the stage in excitement for her special surprise.

Jamie announces that this year's prize will be delivered but first his

must serenade this beautiful woman, with Melvin's approval of

course. Jamie ask Melvin first, "Player before I give her this year's prize can I please serenade your fine lady, and oh yeah, she can be on the album just because." After the crowd laughs again Melvin gives a nod of laughter and appreciation. Jamie then has a chair brought on stage for Angel to sit in as if she was the Queen of the moment. Jamie then begins with, "This is an original I wrote so bare with me. *Girl you know I love you baby, and your heart is shared with mine, Girl you know I'll love you forever, and forever girl you'll always be mine. But on this day I want to know girl, there's a place I want to be. So right now I ask you lady, will you...* "Jamie taps the mic as it seems to have a short. *"Will you..."* the mic goes silent again and Angel is sitting there in awe waiting to here this special song Jamie has wrote. All of a sudden she gets a tap on the shoulder and when she turns around Melvin is on one knee and finishes the question "Marry Me?" Angel breaks out into tears of enjoyment and happily says "Yes!" The crowd goes wild and Melvin and Angel hold each other in tears of joy and excitement and kiss as if they had just gotten married that moment. Not having any idea that Dr. Nobles and Jamie had this set up the whole time, Angel has just been made the happiest women in the world and Dr. Nobles has just made his circle of life complete. As the crowd continues to clap, Angel and Melvin walk off stage for Jamie to continue to entertain the crowd. As they go into the building where they are secluded from the crowd Angel looks at Melvin with her water filled eyes of joy, "Baby, is this real? Do you really want to be with me? I know that we have been through a lot. We have had our ups and downs but I am more than happy to be your wife. I promise that I will never let you down. I will be by your side through thick and…" Melvin places his fingers gently on her lips,"Shhh baby, its ok. I know that you are my completion. You are the reason I rise every morning. I know that you are the one for me and me for you. I just want you to know that out of all the women in the world, you mean the world to me, which makes you the ultimate woman. I feel as if when my heart beats, it beats to the rhythm of your name. I want you to know that from the first time you walked into my office, the breath that I took was finished by your presence, so if we ever part, my oxygen will cease. I will have no reason to live, because you are my breath and for you I exhale. Baby, I am your heart, I am your soul, and I am your everything." Melvin kisses her on her cheek, her forehead, and on her lips, then takes her hand and places it on his heart. "For you I am, and I am, for you."

Chapter 10

A couple of months have passed and the anticipation of the wedding is approaching. Angel is convinced that her soon to be husband has surely forgotten her birthday since February is the shortest month of the year. She feels that it has slipped his mind. Angel moans softly as she wakes up on a beautiful Saturday morning. "Melvin, Melvin?" she calls for her man as she is surprised not to find him lying next to her. "Where are you? Are you in the shower? Melvin? Melvin stop playing!" The house is very quiet and seems at peace. Angel sits up in the bed and stretches real hard and reaches for her silk robe. As she looks to the floor sliding out of their Californian king sized bed, she notices a trail of rose pedals. She begins to follow this path of pedals to the bathroom only to find the marble tub filled with milk body bath, silk rose pedals and candles lit all around. Angel smiles as she removes her robe and slides into the tub. As she is relaxing in the tub she notices next to it a scroll that is tied with a royal purple ribbon. She removes the ribbon and reads the note. *Baby, today is your day. On this 25th day of February, God delivered an Angel to earth. He shaped and molded all that is good in his image and came up with you. To me you are the greatest of all creations. I am glad this day is special, not only because it is your birthday, but because this is the day the world was blessed. I want to and will make this day one of the most memorable of your life. You are my oxygen, my reason to live. You have supported me in every way thus far and today I will show my gratitude. I will forever love you and be your man. I can not wait until the day you become Mrs. Nobles. Once you get ready, I want you to go downtown to the Spa; I got a little something something, there for you. I hope you enjoy. Look behind you and start your day off as luminous as you start mine everyday of the year.* Angel looks behind her and inside a small box is a diamond necklace. "Damn!" She exclaims. "For me to have a man like Melvin, I must be in heaven." Anxious to go on with her day, Angel gets up, puts on her clothes and proceeds to the spa. Once she arrives she is the only customer there. Dr. Nobles has bought out the entire spa just for the employees to cater to his soon to be wife. Angel is speechless. She enjoys an onslaught of pampering and submissiveness from the staff. From therapeutic massages to a nice mud bath, Angel knows she is the Queen for the day. After awhile in the spa, Angel is preparing to leave when all of a sudden one of the staff says, "Excuse me, Ms. Angel, this way please." Angel is baffled. What else it could be, she thinks. The staff member opens a dressing room door and there hangs a beautiful black sequenced dress with splits going up the sides to accentuate Angel's sexy physique. Attached to the dress is a note. *Put this on sweetheart and just wait at the front door.* Angel puts the dress on and tells the staff thank you. As she walks out of the door, surprisingly, there is a beautiful white horse and carriage waiting on her. She is almost in tears at that instant. The driver of the carriage calls out to her "Ms. Angel, on this 25th day of February, your chariot awaits." Angel then proceeds to get into the carriage and enjoys a nice trip through downtown Atlanta. The carriage pulls up to the most exclusive dining establishment in Atlanta owned by one of Atlanta's premier record label owners. This place is one of the hardest to book because of the month long waiting list. You have to be pretty prestigious to get in.

"Oh my God!" Melvin has out done himself today.

As she enters the restaurant, there are rose pedals on the floor that lead to a glass elevator that is exclusive to the owner. This elevator has silk pedals on the floor and takes Angel to a very remote and private area that only the owner himself enjoys. When she steps off the elevator, the owner is standing there with a bottle of his best and ushers Ms. Angel to her seat and tells her happy birthday. As he walks away, Angel is in awe of everything that has happened today. She is wondering to herself, what can top this? All of a sudden, there is a whisper in her ear, "Hello, little mama. I got something for you. Look at this." It was a college picture of the Quiz Bowl Team that they were on together. This immediately brought tears to her eyes as she knew it took Melvin extensive measures to go back and find something this minimal to give to his precious Angel. "Baby, I want you to know that I Melvin A.

Nobles am a man who is complete. You are my completion, my

revolution, my institution. Happy Birthday sweetheart!" He then

gives her a kiss on the forehead, the cheek, and then the lips. While

they are enjoying dinner Angel leans over to Melvin and whispers

in his ear to remind him that they are all alone in this exclusive

section. Melvin smiles with erotic anticipation, but looks as if he

has something already up his sleeve. She knows Melvin is up to

something because every time he has these thoughts he tends to

lick his lips and rub his hands together. He leans over to Angel and

kisses her on the neck real softly with his tender lips and tenderly

sucks on her neck while blowing his warm breath on her. He

nibbles on her ear a little and tantalize behind her ears with the tip

of his tongue. Under the table he takes his hand and slides it

between the split in her dress, slowly reaching between her thighs.

She very casually leans back in this velvet chair and relaxes.

Melvin is blowing his warm breath across her neck while

whispering sweetness in her ear. "Baby you are the truth. You are beautiful. You are the present on your birthday." He then proceeds to bury his hand beneath her thighs and cups his hand lightly against her love nest. As he feels her warmth arise against his palm, he begins to suck on her neck a bit harder but with a soft gentleness and strokes her wetness. "Cum in my hand my love, feel your man rub you into ecstasy. I'll take you there Angel." As he calls her name softly in her ear, her body starts to rock as she feels the urge to explode. While his hands cups her vagina, he takes two fingers to personalize her clitoris with its own stroke. Now his tongue is wrapped around hers and she is about to explode. She belts out to him "I am cumming." He then grabs her clit with his two fingers and squeezes as if he wants to back it up. She tries to move his hand and she wants to cum, he squeezes and rubs to make her insanely ready and sucks on her. She wants to cum,"I...I... I am ready to cum" she gets out in a couple of breaths. He then lets it go and rubs her nest fast as he can.

"O...o...Ohhhhhhh!" she exclaims. She cums hard in his hand. Her thighs shake and open and close like a human fan. She feels all that is wet between her legs. From the anticipation of what is to come and the public display of affection, Angel is aroused more than ever. She stops and looks at Melvin. He licks his lips and rubs his hands and says to her, "Now, your man will finish what he started, let's go." He stands up, and she can see the imprint in his pants that he is a true soldier ready for war and she is ready to be conquered. She tries to get up, but can barely move her legs. So Melvin decides to help her. He removes his jacket and takes a piece of ice and places it in his mouth. Under the table he goes, knowing that his lady is sensitive, cooling down her thighs with the ice held between his teeth. Close to the nest he gets, but only in a teasing like gesture. He gently goes back and forth and cools her thighs down more. After about 6 minutes of ice melting ecstasy, Melvin stands Angel up and carries her to the elevator, out the door, and to the carriage. He places her in the carriage as if her back is to the driver and she is leaning over the back seat, Melvin closes the carriage door. Inside, he slides behind her and rubs his face against her buttocks. He then pulls a feather from his inner suit coat pocket

71

and begins to tantalize her with it softly. He teases her body the entire way to their destination. Once they arrive at their final destination, he carries her inside to the room. He tells her, "I will make a bet with you. I will give you something to read and if you can read this without making a sound, we can move the wedding date to whenever you want. Hell tomorrow if you like, but if I win, it's vice versa." Sure of herself, she agrees, "So be it." "I don't think you know what you just did yourself" he says. The piece that she has to read was written by him earlier that day. He calls it, the guide to winning this bet. The directions state that you must read these aloud.

"Are you ready?" He asked.

"Let's get it!" She begins to read.

"Hold me close. Look into my eyes. Now place your nose on my nose and gaze deeper into my eyes. Lick my lips with your tongue, slowly. Take your hands and place them on my back and rub them down the curve of my spine very slowly. Now suck on my bottom lip gently with your lips. Kiss my neck softly while your hands slowly caress me. Pull me closer so I can feel you against me. Now whisper in my ear something sweet and nasty." Melvin whispers in her ear something that makes her nipples erect like the middle of a cold winters night. "Take my hand and walk me to the bed. Remove my dress slowly. Now lay me down, kiss me on my lips, and then place the blindfold on me." Right then the instructions were complete. Angel is now on the bed with a blindfold ready for anything Melvin has to offer. He takes the feather and slowly rubs against her stomach. He goes back and forth across her chest teasing her nipples with it. He tantalizes her body with this feather until he notices her erotic anticipation arise. He then takes a piece of ice from the bucket and rubs it across her nipples while watching her back arch up into a perfect 's' curve. To give her double the sensation, he takes the feather and slides it between her legs back and forth until she is about to climax. With the ice on her nipples, body stretched out, and the feather sliding back and forth across her throbbing love below, Angel reaches that climatic point. "Melvin, Melvin. Don't stop, don't stop. Oh

Melvin!" she exclaims as loud as the law allows. Her body begins to shiver in the bed with satisfaction. Melvin slowly removes the blindfold, kisses his lady on the lips and says, "I win." She smiles and hugs her pleasuring prince and lays to rest.

Chapter 11

Leaving out of the movies on a warm spring night, Melvin and Angel decide to go to a place called Lookout Mountain. This is a quiet little spot in the hills where couples go parking to relax and get away from the rest of society. Listening to their autographed Jaime Foxx CD all the way to the mountain, the couple rides and grooves silently as if they were on a musical cloud that was floating along. Arriving at their destination, Melvin parks the car, turns the radio down and looks across at his future wife and smiles with all great expectations of the joy marriage will bring. "You know sweetheart, I was at lunch with my partner today. And we were talking about relationships. Now, usually he is comical type of guy but today he made one of the most moving statements that I have ever heard. Now I am not sure if it was because it came from him or because I care for you so much, but can you believe that I was crying at a Pizza Hut, listening to him." Melvin laughs at

75

himself at just the thought of a grown man crying over some pizza while listening to his comical friend talk about relationships, who would have thought." "What happened baby?" Angel asked with all sincerity. "Well," He responded." We were sitting there and one of his favorite songs, *You are my Lady* by Freddie Jackson came on. He started talking about how this was the song that he would get married to. Then he just went into what getting married meant to him. "Now baby, he isn't the type to just settle down with anybody, but his words were so parallel to my thoughts of you, I feel that I got caught up in an emotional state and the thought of combining my heart with yours just overwhelmed me. I was consumed in a love abyss and yes, in front of my boy, I let the tears run down my face." They both began to laugh hysterically. As the laughter came to a minimal, Angel took Melvin's hand and began to speak. "Sweetheart, baby, my love..." She speaks softly and slowly annunciating every word as you can hear the angelic purity sound leaving her lips. "I have always been an independent and strong black woman. I have always found myself proudly standing above ridicule and hatred. When other's doubted me and thought that I would not make it in life, I stood tall as the strong image of my mother. When they talked about me and thought that because of my looks I was promiscuous, I ignored them and worked even harder due to the perseverance instilled in me by my father. I have always had the, 'I don't need a man I can do it by myself mentality,' Though I know a lot of times in life I probably missed out on some things because I focused my attention on the wrong things, but baby I will say this; I am glad that fate led me to you. Not because of your powerful status, but because you are powerful in spirit. Not because you are adored by many, but because you adore me. See a lot of us woman go through life searching for Mr. Right, when most of the time he is right there, we just don't see it. Usually he is the one that we listen to, share secrets with, and occasionally flirt with; only regarding him as a good friend, not realizing he is the perfect compliment. For some reason we as women envision our men comprised of the characteristics that our closest male friend exhibits. Funny though, we never really see our friend like that; placing him in the 'he's like my brother' category. I think it's because we just don't want to mess up a good thing. That is why he remains the friend in our eyes. But…" Melvin interjects "Baby, baby. I don't mean to stop you but are you still talking to me?" With a small chuckle she replies "I'm sorry. I was watching the Oxygen Channel last night and it made me think about how sometimes the best thing is right in front of us, but we are too blind to see it. Baby, I just want to say, I am forever happy that you are here with me. And I want you to love me just as I love you." They lean toward each other, kiss softly and embrace each other. Once the two come up for air and have fogged the windows up with humid passion, Melvin opens the moon roof of the Escalade and he and Angel gaze at the beautiful stars above. "See that sweetheart that is Orion, my favorite constellation. It is said to be the easiest to find as you can find the three stars across the belt." Melvin points to the constellation. "And right there is the big dipper. But the brightest star of all is right…" Melvin slowly points his hand back and forth as Angel follows it, until he slowly comes down to the tip of her noise…"there! You are the brightest star I know. I am lucky and blessed to have a star like you in my life. My father told me that one day I will find that perfect compliment and Angel my dear, there is no other that shall compare." Melvin rubs her cheek bone gently and unlocks the door. Melvin gets out of the SUV and walks around to Angel's door. He opens the door and reaches for his woman. Once she steps out of the car, Melvin uses the remote to play a song that was playing on the radio when Angel first entered his office, "*Together Forever*" by Shai. Angel romantically collapsed in her fiancé arms. From that point on, they dance the night away. It was a perfect setting, the moon was luminous and the stars were winking at the couple. It was the perfect evening to take a deep breath and simply smile.

THOUGHTS of the MIND PART III

Your Relationship vs. Your Friend

It is always the one who has no one to go home to, love, just talk to or ignite his or her fire; that believe they are always right when it comes to relationship advice. Now I know that many of you spend time with your better half, friend, or companion and wonder where this relationship is going to take us. Many people often wonder why they have arguments and will they ever stop? What I am doing wrong? What can I do or we do to better the relationship? These are many questions that all REAL relationships go through. The last person you should seek advice from is your friend that has no one. You know your friend who knows everything about everyone because he or she has nothing else better to do. You know your friend, the one who is so pretty that everyone has tried to talk to them, that is why they remain single. You know your friend who has so many prospects and time on his or her hand that he or she is always trying to fix your relationship. I know that you want to trust and value your friend, thus you listen to their advice. Of course they have YOU in THEIR best interest, which is why they lead you down the path of solitude and singleness. That is why when you get to the end of the road you are the one in tears and they are there to console you. That is why you and YOUR relationship can not work, like the PERFECT one that they are in, because you listened to them, you know again, they are the experts, and they are the ones with no one. Ok now that I have made my point, LISTEN. Every relationship has its up and downs and it is on you to work through them. The problem is lack of COMMUNICATION. People say honesty is the best policy but COMMUNICATION can keep the contract. Lack of communication may break a relationship; ergo it's all about who you communicate with. Sure, your friends have your best interest, but they are not you or your partner. That is their opinion of the situation. But it is just that an OPINION. Only you know how your partner truly feels because they COMMUNICATE this to you, It may be verbal, non-verbal or however, but it's your partner's communication that is the most important. I could really go on and on about this but I want to see what you all have to say and I know you will say a lot. But the bottom line is: STOP LETTING YOUR FRIEND DICTATE AND MESS UP A PERFECTLY GOOD THING. Because in the end you will be by yourself trying to figure out what happened. Then you will be just like your friend; lonely and bitter, ruining the next person's relationship. Is that what you want?

Chapter 12

"Boy you a fool! I know you and I know how you do it. I'm just trying to have a little fun but not too much fun, or better yet your fun." Melvin states to his best friend, as they have a phone conversation about the bachelor party. "Alright boy, I will see you tonight about 7pm, cool." Melvin hung up the phone with laughter. Thinking to himself about tonight's bachelor party as he drives home, he calls his lovely bride to be.

"Hello baby. What you doing?"

"Nothing, just reading a book," She replies.

"Oh yeah, what is it about?" he asked.

"Well, it's about this young woman who falls for an older man, but she is torn between admitting her love for him and realizing that he is too old for her." "Wow, how old is he? And what do they do?" Melvin inquires. "The young woman is 20 and in college and the man is 32 and he is a professional athlete. I think they met at a club. But it seems that she is mature and carries herself well and he is really feeling her. His teammates get on him time to time about her, but it seems that the feelings are genuine." Angel responds as if she was writing the book. Melvin ponders the scenario and asks, "So what is the problem. When people are in their 40's and 50's no one seems to care, but it seems like at that age, it's so wrong. Why is that baby? If he feels for her and she feels for him, then it should be what it is. But you and I know that some people just will not look past their own blinders and use any excuse as a reason to hate." Angel begins to laugh. "Damn Melvin, you act like that is you or something. I understand baby, I really do." Laughing to himself Melvin responds "You right baby, it is what it is. Anyway, my boys are throwing me a bachelor party tonight and I just wanted to assure you nothing will happen and everything is going to be strictly hands off. I don't want you to think that..." abruptly Angel stops Dr. Nobles in his plea, "Baby, I already know. You are a great man and I have no inclination in my bones that you would do anything to boil my blood, especially on the eve of our wedding consummation. This is one of the many reasons I am marrying you. Even on the eve of our wedding day, your last night out as a single man, and your last single day to do whatever you feel, you think of me and my feelings Dr. Nobles for that I love you and trust you 200%. You don't have to tell me a word. You enjoy your bachelor party and your friends." Feeling like a breath of fresh air, Dr. Nobles simply smiles and says, "Thank you. That is why I love you because you are so understanding" He then hangs up the phone and drives home with a smile.

Later that night at a private location, the fellas are all gathered around having a great time. The men are all called into this great big master room. The room has one big white luxury fur love seat in the middle where Melvin is placed. All of a sudden there is announcement that hushes the crowd. "Attention Fellas! Now is the time that you all have been waiting for. Introducing an All-star lineup, here they are the lovely ladies of seduction; Perfect Margarita, Alize, E&J, Hypnotiq, Malibu, Hennessey, Grey Goose,

Passion Fruit, Gin, Juice, and Tanqueray. For your viewing pleasure pull your money out and keep your funny in. O my lawd, the Chevy's a monster!" All of a sudden 11 of the most beautiful women you have ever laid eyes on appeared from the room. Every jaw in the building dropped as they gazed in amazement. Three of the finest women approached Melvin as he sat on his love seat of seduction. Each one greeting him with erotic movements as they each whispered in his ear seductively. "Would you like a taste of Alize?" "Would you like to put your hands on this Hypnotiq body?" "Can you handle a Perfect Margarita?" The center of jealous attention right now, Dr. Nobles is surrounded by the most beautiful women one has ever seen and yet he is emotionless and dry with non excitement. The ladies dance, tease, and tantalize Dr. Nobles with everything they got, but he is as stubborn as the last driver to turn at a traffic light when you are in a rush; HE AINT MOVING. Hypnotiq leans over Melvin with her perfect body and whispers "tell me what you want and it shall be yours." Melvin sits up straight, leans toward Hypnotiq and says softly, "Angel and I already have everything I could possibly want", then leans back and smiles. The ladies then proceed to move away from Melvin and work the rest of the crowd as the rest of the men were excited to be present. After the entertainment was over Melvin was sitting off in a corner by himself. One of the young ladies who had been dancing earlier comes over to Melvin and says "You know sweetheart, in all my years of dancing, I've never seen a man as loyal and committed as you. I don't know who she is but I do know that she has to be one of the luckiest ladies in the world because you are truly in love." As she speaks to Melvin a tear rolls down her face. "You are a blessing to the world and may you have a blessed marriage. You are the essence of a man." She leans over and places a kiss on his cheek and walks away.

Melvin gets home and picks up the phone. He thinks to himself before he dials the number where his life will be headed as tomorrow comes near. Melvin thinks to himself about what he has done thus far in life and what he still wants to accomplish. His mind is at a tranquil state when it comes to his pure thoughts of the woman who he will soon call his wife. As Melvin ponders the thought of his life with his future wife, he breathes easily and is satisfied with what the future holds. Dialing her number, Angel answers the phone with a whispering tone, "Hello, Melvin what are you doing? You know its bad luck to speak to each other the night before the wedding." Angel is at her sister's house with all her friends and family, hiding away in the bathroom. Melvin replies, "First of all sweetheart we are not suppose to see each other, speaking to each other is fine." he says with a small chuckle. "I see you every time I blink or close my eyes, because you are constantly with me. You are my heart. Baby, I just had to call you and say I love you and I can not wait to spend the rest of my life with you. I would spend two lifetimes with you if I could. Everything I ever wanted is embedded in you. Everything I ever needed is satisfied by your love. I just had to call you and tell you I love you." Blushing from ear to ear Angel expresses to Melvin, "Tomorrow I will become Mrs. Angel Nobles. This will be the greatest moment of my life. I have always dreamed of the day a man would come into my life and be everything I want. Not only are you everything I want, you are everything I need." Tears of joy begin to run down her cherubic cheek bones as she tells her future husband how she feels. "You have been my rock and my salvation ever since the day I walked into your office. I know sometimes it's difficult to tolerate me, but you have done so nonetheless. I know at times that I can be spoiled with my attitude, but you always find a way to turn that into sunshine. I use to worry in school about what people said about me. I use to feel as if I got certain things in life because of my looks and not who I was. Dr. Nobles, I must say that you have shown me the way. You have appreciated me for who I am and what makes me whole. I love you too baby and cant wait to marry you tomorrow. The wedding bells are already ringing and the birds are singing. I can lay here and talk to you all night." Angel wipes her tears away and thinks of her future husband and goes to sleep. Melvin thinks of his beautiful future and falls asleep on the phone with his wife to be.

Chapter 13

The wedding day is here. The sun is out, the birds are singing, and business is great. By now, S.H.I.T is the number one corporation in America. Stocks are up, investors are happy, and the product is good. This is the greatest day in Melvin's life. Nothing can ruin this day. The church is packed and the Pastor Emory LL. Lightfoot Jr. will be the one to anoint Melvin and Angel into this marriage. As Melvin stands on the alter with his white suit trimmed in royal purple, matching the carpet and the colors of his surroundings, this beautiful image of God's creation is walking down the isle to her soon to be husband. Angel looks as precious as the day she walked into his office. As she approaches the altar, Melvin's eyes began to fill up with tears of joy and appreciation. Once Angel actually arrives at the altar, both she and Dr. Nobles eyes are fixated on one another with love and admiration beaming from within. As they transition through the wedding procession, the time comes to recite the vows written by each one of them. But as Angel begins to read hers, Melvin does something out of the ordinary. He places his finger on her mouth and says, "Baby, my lady, my friend." As tears run down his face, "Your vows are my vows. Your wishes are my wishes. Every thought you begin, I will end. There is no need for you to read your vows because they are already written on my heart. I told you before that you are my and I am your completion. All my life I have wanted and needed to breathe. You are the oxygen I live for. My vow to you is to complete and unify you in my spirit. I want to be and will be the bottom of your feet when you walk, and the comfort of your heart when you lay. I am you and you are me. My vow is to be your vow." As Angel cries tears of happiness, they both wipe each others tears away. There is not a dry eye in the church. The rings are placed and the ceremony is complete. "You may kiss your bride" the Reverend exclaims. After the two kiss, Mr. and Mrs. Nobles walk down the aisle into the light of happiness. Right as they approach the door. Melvin looks at his woman and picks her up off of her feet and carries her to the carriage that waits. As Melvin places his lady in the carriage and waives to the crowd, Angel does not wave. Something is wrong, the crowd has a sudden calm over them and Angel does not move. Dr. Nobles begins to panic. "Angel, Angel, wake up sweetheart. Please!" Melvin yells "Someone call 911, please damn it, someone call now!" Angel is not responding. The ambulance arrives and immediately places Angel on the stretcher and into the ambulance. Melvin jumps in his car with his best friend and follows the ambulance to the hospital. The crowd is in shock because this joyous occasion has just turned tragic. Melvin arrives at the hospital and runs into the emergency room to find out what his bride is going through. He sees the doctors through the window trying to revive her, but he does not know what is wrong. Melvin is frantic and damn near hysterical. The nurse has to call back up just to calm him down and make him go to the waiting area. "That's my damn wife, that's my wife. Angel!" He shouts. "Angel, Angel! That's my wife in the there." He turns to his best friend. "That's my wife in there man, that is my wife." Melvin begins to breakdown in his best friends arms. Like a man who has lost the world. "That's my wife!" Sadly he exclaims.

After an hour passes the doctor comes out, "Mr. Nobles.

"Yes sir," Melvin answers. "That's me. How is my wife? How is she? Where is she? Is she coming out soon? She was just nervous huh? I know she probably fainted that's all. Today is our wedding day you know. How is my wife, that's my wife you know?" Melvin is babbling out of nervousness. "Sir, Sir", the doctor tries to get Melvin's attention. "Sir, listen to me. First of all, sit down. She is not dead or anything like that. She is with us and she will be alright, eventually."

"Eventually?" Melvin asked.

The doctor proceeds, "Yes sir, your wife is in a coma. She has suffered a very bad kidney failure which has triggered a chain reaction throughout the body. I don't know how long she will be in this coma, but we have to find someone who can and will donate a kidney to her." Melvin sits down with a bewildered and helpless expression on his face. Once regaining his composure, Melvin

looks up at the doctor with red watery eyes and says to him, "I will

do it. I will be the one."

Chapter 14

A couple of days have gone by and Melvin is driving himself berserk. Worried for the life of his new wife and precious gift, he drops to his knees and prays. "Lord, why have you forsaken me? I have done all that you asked of me. I have tried so hard to be a good man. I have tried to emulate you in all that I do. Why now Lord? What have I done to deserve this?" Melvin drops his head and begins to cry. "I just don't understand. All my life I have been a good man. I have worked hard and prayed even harder. I have motivated, educated, and lived my life accordingly. I finally find the perfect compliment and she is taken from me. Why now Lord, why now?" Melvin gets up in a furious rage as if the image of God was before him. "Why?" He begins to yell. "What have I done to you? Is this not the way you want me to live? Do I not deserve this woman of greatness? Please, Please tell me why?" In a blind rage he begins to destroy the furniture in the house. He turns over the couch, throws the lamp against the wall, and punches several holes in the wall. "Damn you, damn you God! Why have you forsaken me?" Melvin then drops to his knees and places his face in his hands and begins to cry. He feels as if his whole life has been for nothing. He begins to slump down until he is face down on the floor. Melvin cries his self to sleep.

During the night as Melvin sleeps, he tosses and turns while on the floor and has a crazy dream. *"Where am I? Where is everybody? Angel where are you? I can't see anything. What am I doing here?"* A light begins to shine in Melvin's face. He hears a familiar soothing voice but sees no one. *"Baby, I am with you. I have always been with you. I am not going anywhere. Why are you so sad? Be strong my love and remember to breathe. You know that our heartbeat is one and our circle is complete. I am right here walking and talking with you."* Melvin asks, *"Where are you? I can't see you? Are you ok?"* The voice responds but is fading, *"I am here my love. I have not gone anywhere. Be strong and believe in me as I have believed in you."* The voice has faded and the light grows dim. Melvin is confused and running around in circles in the dark. He begins to yell. *"Hello! Hello! Is anybody there? Hello! What can I do? What shall I do?"* He falls to his knees.

Waking up about two hours later, he gets up off the floor and slowly walks to the restroom. He turns on the hot water in the sink and places his face towel in the water. Once it is hot enough for him, he places the towel onto his face. After splashing the water a few times in his face, Melvin looks in the mirror. He gazes for a second as if he is trying to solve a mystery. Slowly he begins to pray softly and methodically. "I know you have a plan for me and my wife. I know through all things your mercy is upon me. It is hard sometimes in this life not knowing why, what, or how come. But I do realize you are my light and my salvation. There is nothing that you would place on me, if you did not think I could bear it. My faith in you has not changed and I am sorry for the things that I have said. The things I said were out of anger. It seems that sometimes in our lives we feel that we're are the only ones that go through trials and tribulations, but we are not. All we have to do is call upon you; not just in our time of need, but to give you your needed time." Melvin falls to his knees and folds his hands and looks up to the heavens above. "Father, guide me and forgive me. For I realize now, that with you and through you, all things will be saved."

THOUGHTS of the MIND Part IV

The Perfect Relationship

I feel that during your first couple of years in college, relationships should be the last thing on your mind. But if you must, I feel that a relationship is founded on trust, faith, and respect. A man and a woman should complete each other in every way. I feel as if when you are together you are not just with the one you love, but that you grow with the one you love. When you inhale, your mate exhales. Your heart beats the same pattern and your thought processes are parallel to one another. Sure you will have your downs, but your ups will balance them out and beyond. I would want for my woman to be able to just breathe and feel as if she is the light of the world, and as long as I exist she will always shine. In a good relationship everything will even itself out. You will finish her sentences. Not only will you walk beside her but you will walk with her and grow with her. Love is not just a physical thing, but more of an emotional sentiment. See, in a good relationship, if your emotions and mental compatibilities feel balanced then everything else will proceed. To think of your mate and cry to yourself just because of the joy she brings you, is love. To whisper her name at night when you sleep or to hold the phone with her the whole night while you both sleep is love. When you find someone that can make all or most of these things happen, then in my opinion, you have the perfect relationship.

Chapter 15

Two weeks have passed and the results are back in from the doctor's office. Melvin has been contacted and told that he is a perfect donor match, but the doctor has requested to speak with Melvin about some issues. Melvin arrives at the hospital and proceeds into the doctor's office. He tells the nurse at the reception desk, "Yes maam, I am Dr. Nobles here to see Dr. Gabrielle." "Ok sir, I will let him know that you are here to see him. Please have a seat until he is available." The nurse replies to Melvin. While he waits, Melvin places his face in his hands and calls on his true doctor." Dear God, I have tried to live my life right by your name. I have worked hard all my life and have been Christian like. I have always praised you and tried to live in your image. If there is anything I ever needed, it is your healing power right now Lord. Though I do not know why on my wedding day you did the things you did, but I know you have a plan for us. Dear God, please spare my wife, I will do anything in your name, just to have my baby speak to me. I feel breathless without her. Lord, be kind and merciful to her as you ultimately are. I ask this in your name, Amen." Just as Melvin finishes praying to himself, Dr. Gabrielle calls him to the office. "Sit down son. Listen; there are a few things you must know. What your wife has endured is reversible, but this is not a routine kidney transplant procedure. She needs the transplant to be able to live and hopefully bring her out of her coma, but I must warn you that the donor is taking a 50/50 risk on themselves. To be honest with you, this specific procedure can be dangerous to the donor. A certain malfunction of the kidney can cost the donor and be detrimental to their health, even causing sudden death. Again, your wife will be revived through the operation, but please understand it is a life changing decision." Melvin replies to the doctor in a calm and methodical tone, "Have you ever loved someone so much that you will go to the ends of the earth for them? Have you ever been in a situation where you could not breathe and you were fighting for that last amount of oxygen and were relieved when you got it? Do you know that one flower in the garden that stands out above the rest no matter what season it is? Doctor these things represent Angel. She is the truth in every question. She is the beauty in every picture and the sound in every song that makes it beautiful. My love for her can not be measured by anything except a higher being. There is nothing I would not do for my peach. She truly is a gift from above. I thank you for your honesty and concern, but this is not an option. It is my duty and responsibility as her husband and as the man that I am." Melvin looks the doctor in his eyes and Dr. Gabrielle just shakes his head with affirmation as he understands completely Melvin's thoughts about his woman. "Ok Melvin, the operation will be next Thursday at 9am. I will see you then." Melvin stands up, shakes the doctors' hand then proceeds out of the office.

As Melvin gets back to his office he goes back to the window and reminisces back to the day when Angel first walked in. He chuckles to himself as he remembers how he bumbled and baffled through sentences. He remembered that precious glow she had on her face. Melvin remembers looking out of his office and being mystified by her presence. Now, he must give a part of himself for her to continue that beautiful smile. Sitting in his chair Melvin thinks of all the wonderful things that he and his wife will do together. He gets on the phone and books a cruise to the Caribbean Islands on a private resort. He sets all of this up for the two of them to enjoy a long awaited honeymoon. Feeling like a brand new man and elated his wife will soon be coming home, Melvin hops up with joy and goes home to celebrate. On the way home Melvin stops at the number one diamond store in Atlanta and has a diamond necklace costumed made to say "ANGEL" with 100 diamonds in it. Melvin is so excited at the thought of Angel's home-coming, that he is ready for the operation. Each day, Melvin counts down the days to the operation, with thoughts of the lifetime he will spend with his new bride.

The night before the operation, Melvin cannot sleep. The anticipation of his wife coming home after recovering from surgery is so great that he has redecorated the house and set everything up perfect. He calls his secretary's voicemail reminding her that he will be out of the office until further notice due to the procedure. Finally, at about 2am Melvin falls asleep.

Operation day is here! Melvin arrives at the hospital and checks in with the Doctor. He goes into a room to remove his clothes, slides into a hospital robe, then proceeds down a long cold hallway until he reaches the operating room. Slowly, he walks through the doors of the O.R. and views his lovely wife lying on the table motionless. There is an empty operating table next to her for him to lie on. Melvin looks at the doctor with confidence and nods his head with approval. He lies on the table next to his woman, and before he receives his dose of anesthesia, he reaches out and grabs her hand and says, "My Angel, you are truly a delivery from heaven and when we both awaken, we will be as one." The doctor places the anesthesia over Melvin's face and he is out. The doctor is meticulous during the surgery. After 3 hours the surgery is coming to completion, but something is wrong. The heart monitor begins to slow down. "Something is wrong!" the doctor exclaims. "There has been a shutdown in the kidney system. It's nothing we can control; I was afraid of this." As the room becomes silent, all you can hear is one of the heartbeat monitors slowing down. Angel and Melvin's eyes both open slowly out of their slumber, gazing at each other. With Angel not knowing she has been in a coma and Melvin happy to see his sweetheart, neither of them notice the heartbeat monitor slowing down. Angel deeply inhales, almost gasping for air as she turns to reach over for Melvin's hand, which he extends out to her. And when their hands join... he exhales and flat lines. Melvin has passed.

Chapter 16

Melvin opens his eyes, and exhales slowly as he looked across the streets of Atlanta. Confused, he looks at the door to await the knock, but it never came. Where is Angel? Where is Dr. Gabrielle? What happened during the surgery? Melvin sits down in his chair and looks out his window. He takes a deep breath once again and exhales slowly, then realizes that he was only thinking to himself what a companion would be like; it was all a day dream. He was dreaming of an angel to be delivered to him the whole time. Dr. Nobles begins to laugh whole heartedly as he looks out of his window. "What a dream? It seemed so real!" he exclaimed to himself. Melvin sits back and just gazes out of the window. A whole work day has passed and it is time to go home. As Melvin shuts his computer down and closes his blinds, there is a knock at the door. "Come in!" he says. "Excuse me, excuse me. I am looking for Dr. Melvin A. Nobles. They said that I could find him up here. Are you Dr. Nobles, Sir?", a young woman says. He turns around slowly as if he has heard a ghost. There entered the most beautiful woman he had ever laid his eyes on. She stood about 5'3, pecan red tan, hazel eyes, micro braids, and a pair of legs that were so bowlegged; it looked like she was riding a horse. Her skin was honey glazed and a voice soft as a whisper. This was a true delivery from heaven.

The End

Acknowledgements

As always, I would like to thank the Father, the Son, and the Holy Spirit, for giving me the opportunity and blessings to live my life on the right path as I continue to mentor and touch the lives of many so that one day those who are affected will continue to live their lives in the path of the light that you have placed before us.

To all my friends close and far away; I have so many people I could name that it would be another book. Starting from Anniston Alabama to Lakeland Florida to Jacksonville Florida to Miami Florida to Macon Georgia to Fort Valley Georgia. You may not think so but I remember you all and love you all. There are so many who have stood by my side and even there are those who have doubted me thus made me stronger.

I would like to thank everyone who has read, is reading, and will read my book. Thank you for your support, whether it is negative or positive it is all a blessing.

Last but not least I would like to acknowledge the woman. I acknowledged the woman who has always been the support system to her man. I praise the woman who gets yelled at, blamed, and ridiculed for every little thing in a relationship and takes it in stride without ever complaining. I commend the hardworking woman who goes above and beyond the call of duty to not only help provide for her family but sometimes solely provide for her family. I praise the woman who has been called out of her named, abused mentally, abused physically, and tormented but still remained strong. I acknowledge the woman for being a woman of essence, beauty, grace, and style. I recognize and understand that if it were not for womanhood then manhood would not exist. I hope to one day find that special lady that I can call my own and treat as my Angel. I hope to be able to captivate the very emotion of what true love and its existence is all about. I hope to one day be able to say that I have truly found my perfect compliment. But until that day comes, I will forever acknowledge, respect, and praise, the woman and the essence that she is as I would love to exhale too!

Made in the USA
Charleston, SC
05 December 2016